Have You Ever Heard a Hummingbird Hum?

Have You Ever Heard a Hummingbird Hum?

A Colorful Cavalcade of God's Feathery Friends

Bernadette McCarver Snyder

Illustrations by
Jim Richter

AVE MARIA PRESS Notre Dame, Indiana 46556

Dedication

I dedicate this book to William Daniel Snyder, also known as Will, with the hope that he will enjoy meeting these feathered flyers who are fleet, friendly, and fun—just like he is.

International Standard Book Number: 0-87793-631-5

Cover and text design by Elizabeth J. French

Cover and text illustrations by Jim Richter

Printed and bound in the United States of America.

Library of Congress Cataloging-in-Publication Data

Snyder, Bernadette McCarver.
     Have you ever heard a hummingbird hum? : a colorful cavalcade of God's   feathery friends / Bernadette McCarver Snyder.
         p.   cm.
     Summary: Describes features that make various birds that God has created special and suggests how these birds can inspire the reader.
     ISBN 0-87793-631-5
     1. Birds—Religious aspects—Christianity—Juvenile literature.
2. Creation—Juvenile literature.   [1. Birds.   2. Christian life.]   I. Title.
BS664.S59   1997
242'.62—dc21   97-19008
                                                                   CIP
                                                                   AC

Contents

Introduction: God Made WHAT? 7

Have You Ever Heard a Hummingbird Hum? 8

The Mysterious Gypsy Waxwing 10

The Airplane-Submarine Bird 12

A City Bird That Knows How to Sew! 14

The Kookaburra with the Kooky Laugh 16

The Woodpecker and Her Checkerboard 18

The Far-Sighted Flyer 20

Somethin' Lovin' from the Oven 22

This Big Bird Is a Record Holder! 24

Did You Ever See a Blue-Footed Booby? 26

The Nervous Mud Pie Maker 28

Who Wears a Tuxedo to Go Sledding? 30

Taking a Bath with Ants? 32

The Drummer with a Mustache 34

The Condominium Martins 36

The Secret Hideaway Surprise 38

The "Good Luck" Bird 40

Who-o-o Said That? 42

One Good Tern Deserves Another!. 44

The Trash Collector. 46

Beep! Beep! 48

The Curly-Haired Curassow 50

Who Ever Heard of a Secretary Bird? 52

The Decorator Weaver. 54

The Acrobat Bird. 56

Here Comes a Parade! 58

The Dive Bomber Borrower Bird. 60

The Parking Lot Bird. 62

The Blue Bower Builder. 64

The Showoff "Fan Club" 66

Funny Fowl Facts. 68

Introduction

God Made WHAT?

When God made birds, he must have smiled. He gave them feathers and wings and taught them how to fly and how to sing! He painted them with lots of colors—red, blue, yellow, purple, black, and brown.* He made some spotted or speckled. And he made them in every size from itsy-bitsy, teeny-tiny to tall-wild-and-wonderful.

Maybe you have seen some of the birds God made—the robins and wrens, the sparrows and starlings. But have you ever seen a bird with a black mustache or a bird with big blue feet? Have you ever met a long-tailed tailorbird or a curly-headed curassow, a secretary bird or a sapsucker?

Have you ever seen a bird's nest as tiny as a thimble or a nest made from a leaf and lined with spider silk?

Have you ever heard the ghostly cry of a loon or the shriek of a kookaburra? Have you ever heard a hummingbird hum?

You'll meet and read about and see all of those birds—and many other feathered friends—in this book. You may be surprised to learn that God made so many different kinds of "flyers" (just like he made so many different kinds of people!).

Turn the page now and discover how God has filled your world and decorated the skies with his amazing and amusing, exotic and exciting "cavalcade of feathery friends"!

*You'll notice that this book is in black and white—but if you want to make it more colorful, there's a note on each page to suggest which colors you could add.

Hummingbird

Have You Ever Heard a Hummingbird Hum?

A hummingbird flies so fast, you have to look quick to see one! And she can fly forward, backward, straight up or down, sideways—or even hover like a helicopter! But a hummingbird does NOT hum. She can't even carry a tune. She would never be asked to join a bird band or go on TV as a singing sensation. She's called a "humming" bird because her wings move SO FAST, they make a humming sound. God gave this tiny bird wings that can flap about 80 times per second!

The hummingbird needs a lot of energy so she won't feel "beat" after doing all that wing-beating. She gets her energy by sucking the sweet nectar from flowers—the way you might sip an ice cream soda through a straw. The hummer especially likes bright red blossoms, and she flits from flower to flower, eating every ten to fifteen minutes from dawn to dusk! (Can you imagine having to eat that often every day?)

The Cuban "bee hummingbird" is the smallest bird in the world. And the "lady hummer" lays the smallest eggs (about the size of a tiny jelly bean!) and builds the smallest nest (about as big as a thimble!).

How fast can you flap YOUR "wings"? Ask someone to time you today. Flap your arms up and down as fast as you can and see how many times you can flap them in ten seconds . . . or thirty seconds . . . or one minute. Now pretend you are a hummingbird, flitting and humming around the yard, looking for red flowers, flying backward, forward, and sideways.

Then hover awhile and tell God thanks for giving the hummingbird wings that can hover like a helicopter and giving YOU legs that can run, arms that can flap, and a voice that can hum a happy tune!

Hummingbirds come in many colors, but this one has a red head and green wings.

The Mysterious Gypsy Waxwing

Like a band of happy gypsies who wander about the countryside and then suddenly gather in a town, the cedar waxwings come and go mysteriously. They often travel in flocks of forty and like to stop where there are berry bushes or fruit trees.

God gave this pretty bird yellow feathers on his tummy and tail tip—and a mysterious black "mask" to wear around his eyes. But the waxwing got his name from the red wax-like "drips" of color that are on his wing feathers.

The waxwing will eat flies or caterpillars, but his favorite foods are cherries, grapes, and strawberries. And he REALLY feasts when he finds a bird feeder full of raisins and pieces of apple.

Color the tummy and tail tip yellow—and add some red wax drips to the wings.

But here's a surprise . . . The waxwings like to SHARE their food! Two or more will sit quietly on a branch and pass a cherry or flower petal back and forth until they eat it up.

Did you ever see birds share food that way? Do YOU like to share your food? Why don't you get a snack today and then find a friend to share it? While you're eating, you can talk about this interesting bird God made—with a yellow tummy and tail tip, drips of waxy red, and a black mask!

Cedar Waxwing

The Airplane-Submarine Bird

Of course you know that birds can fly, but did you know that some of them can swim too? Of all the birds, the loon is the best swimmer and the deepest diver. And God taught him how to stay underwater longer than any other bird—so he's a little like a submarine!

There is only one problem. The loon can't "take off" like most birds. He has to run along in the water and sometimes he has to run a lo-o-ong way before he gets up enough speed to take off—just like an airplane has to get up speed on the runway at the airport. And when the loon is ready to land, he needs a landing strip of water. But he doesn't come down easy like an airplane. He lands with a great flop and splash!

The loons like the water better than land, but they DO make nests and lay eggs on land. When the eggs hatch, the parents take the baby loons into the water—by letting the babies ride on the

The loon is black and white, so color the water blue.

backs of the parents! The babies know they are safe, riding along on the big loons, and soon the babies get used to the water and they start swimming too!

Do you like to swim or play in the water? The next time you and your friends run through the sprinkler in your yard or splash each other with the hose, pretend you are a combination airplane-submarine like the loon. And while you are "taking off" like a plane or diving like a submarine, tell God thanks for making water and sunshine for you to enjoy and birds like that loon for you to learn about.

Loon

A City Bird That Knows How to Sew!

The long-tailed tailorbird likes to live right in the middle of a busy, noisy, bustling town or city. And God taught the lady tailorbird how to make a wonderful city nest!

She finds a leaf or a cluster of leaves that she likes—and sometimes she chooses a leaf right in the middle of a potted plant! Then, using her fine

Tailorbird

pointed bill like a needle, she makes holes along the leaf edges. Next, she finds spider silk and uses this like "thread" to sew the leaf or leaves together, stitching back and forth through the holes she has made. Soon she has made a little cocoon—with a "door" at the top.

Finally the tailor lady lines her cozy cocoon with fine grass or feathers and has a tailor-made home ready for her eggs. And then guess what happens? When the eggs hatch, the babies have a tailor-made CRADLE! Since the mama bird made her nest in a leaf, the wind blows the leaf back and forth, and it rocks like a cradle or a rocking chair. So the baby birds get rocked just like baby children do!

Do you have a rocking chair in your house? Or do you like to swing in a swing in the park? The next time you rock or swing, think about the little tailorbirds. And the next time you see someone sewing—your mother or grandmother or a friend—tell the sewer about how God made the tailorbird and how the mother tailorbird sews her nest.

Color the leaf nest green and the head of the "tailor" brown.

The Kookaburra with the Kooky Laugh

Kookaburra

Did you ever see a movie about an adventure in the African jungle? In some of those movies, you will see wild animals and beautiful tropical flowers, and THEN you will hear a bird's call that sounds like a loud, shrieking cackle. Well, that kooky laugh is made by the kookaburra. But do you want to know something funny?

The movie-makers like to use that bird's call because they like the sound, but they have to use a RECORDING of the bird's call—because the kookaburra actually lives in Australia and NOT in Africa!

The kookaburra is a member of the kingfisher family and the kingfishers have very unusual homes. They don't build nests in trees or look for a nice, snug birdhouse. Oh no! Using their bills and claws, they shovel dirt out of the steep sides of riverbanks, making a long, narrow tunnel. At the end of the tunnel they make a round hollowed-out "room" to use as a nest. (It takes them about two weeks to build such a home.)

Have YOU ever tried to dig dirt with a shovel? Can you imagine digging a tunnel using your nose and your fingernails? Of course you don't NEED to dig a tunnel to make a house. That's why God gave the kingfisher a strong bill and claws but gave YOU a nose and fingernails!

Put your fingernails (and your fingers) together today and say a prayer to thank God for your home. Aren't you lucky to have a bed to sleep in, food to eat, and a roof to keep out the rain? Imagine what kind of home you would like to have someday. Would you like to live in a big mansion or in a treehouse or on a beach or in an igloo or maybe even at the end of a tunnel? Or would you like to live in Australia so you could hear the cackle of a kookaburra? It's fun to dream about tomorrow but always remember to enjoy—and thank God for—what you have today.

Color this bird's tummy feathers light brown.

The Woodpecker and Her Checkerboard

Did you know God taught the woodpecker how to make checkerboards? He did!

If you ever hear a tap-tapping in your yard—like somebody knocking on your door—look out and you might see a red-headed, yellow-bellied bird busily making a checkerboard on one of your trees. This noisy woodpecker uses her bill to drill lines going across and lines going down, to make squares like you see on a checkerboard. She eats the inner layer of the

Woodpecker

tree bark and then sucks out the sap (which is like tree juice). And that's why she is called a yellow-bellied sapsucker! Isn't that a funny name?

To balance her diet, this woodpecker also likes to eat holly berries, elderberries, suet, and grape jelly! Of course, she can't shop for suet and grape jelly on her own, so she has to find a friendly bird-lover who will kindly put those goodies into a bird feeder.

Do you have a bird feeder in YOUR yard? It's fun to put out seeds and leftover bread and bits of fruit for the birds to enjoy. Some birds like peanut butter—and THIS bird likes grape jelly. Do YOU like peanut butter and jelly?

Why don't you have a peanut butter and jelly sandwich today and think about what chores you could do to make enough money to buy a bird feeder to put in your back yard? Or maybe you might like to buy some binoculars so you could become a bird-watcher instead of a bird-feeder. Or you might like to turn the page and learn some more about the many fine-feathered birds God made!

You know what to color this bird—the head red and the tummy yellow!

The Far-Sighted Flyer

This bird is called the bald eagle—but he isn't really bald. His head is covered in white feathers, but most of the rest of him is covered in dark feathers, so when you see him from a distance he LOOKS like his head is bald. And you DO often see him from a long distance because God made the eagle a HIGH flyer. He can fly higher than almost any other bird. But even though he is way up in the sky, the eagle can see something way down on the ground. He can spot food a mile away! That is REALLY being far-sighted.

Eagle

An eagle will soar through the sky on broad wings and then swoop down to catch his dinner faster than you could eat a cookie! And then he might soar back home to his nest which is built very high and is called an aerie.

Although you will probably never see a real bald eagle in your neighborhood, you will see lots of pictures of this high flyer because the bald eagle is the official bird of the United States, and his picture is on the Great Seal of America. You might see this seal on an official building or in a Fourth of July parade—OR you could see one today. Do you have a $1 bill? If you don't, ask someone to let you look at his or her $1 bill! You'll see a picture of George Washington on the front, but if you look at the back of the bill, you won't have to be far-sighted to spot the picture of the bald eagle!

The next time you have a $1 bill of your own, think about the eagle and then think of what you could do with that $1—not for yourself but for somebody else! Could you buy a surprise present for someone in your family? Could you give away the $1 to your church or to someone who really needs it? What ELSE could you do with $1? Be far-sighted and think of ALL the little things you could do with $1 to surprise or please somebody. And then do one of those things soon!

Color the eagle's beak yellow—and also his far-sighted eye!

Somethin' Lovin' from the Oven

Did you ever hear of the ovenbird? He's called that because he builds a strange nest out of mud or clay, and when the nest is finished it looks like the old-fashioned clay ovens that people once used to bake bread!

During the wet winter months the little ovenbirds look around and find a place to build a new home—usually in a tree or on a fence post. Then they get to work and start putting together lumps of mud or clay, a little bit at a time. They add twigs or grass to hold the nest together, and when the sun comes out it bakes the clay hard. The birds keep adding to it until it is like a round ball with a hole in one side for the "front door."

It takes a lot of hard work for these little birds. They must carry between 1,500 and 2,000 lumps of clay to get the nest big enough, and when it is finished it weighs from seven to twelve pounds—as much as some bowling balls!

The mommy bird lines the oven-nest with soft grass and feathers, and it is very warm and cozy inside. Because it has been baked hard by the sun, the nest is strong enough to last for two or three years, but the ovenbirds build a new nest every year.

Other birds in the ovenbird family have interesting names too—the castlebuilder, the plainsrunner, the leafgleaner, and the thistletail.

Aren't you glad that instead of living in an oven-house, you live in a house that just has an oven in the kitchen? Why don't you ask a grown-up in your family to let you help bake something this week? Maybe you could make cookies or brownies—or a big batch of spinach and eggplant and rutabaga hash! Whatever you decide to make or bake, when you sit down to eat it say a blessing to thank God for all the good things you like best—and for little birds who build oven-nests.

Color the bird's head and back light brown, like the color of the top of a loaf of baked bread.

Ovenbird

This Big Bird Is a Record Holder!

The ostrich holds the record as the world's BIGGEST bird. She can run faster than any other two-legged animal. She lays the largest eggs of any living creature. And she's like a karate champion because she fights

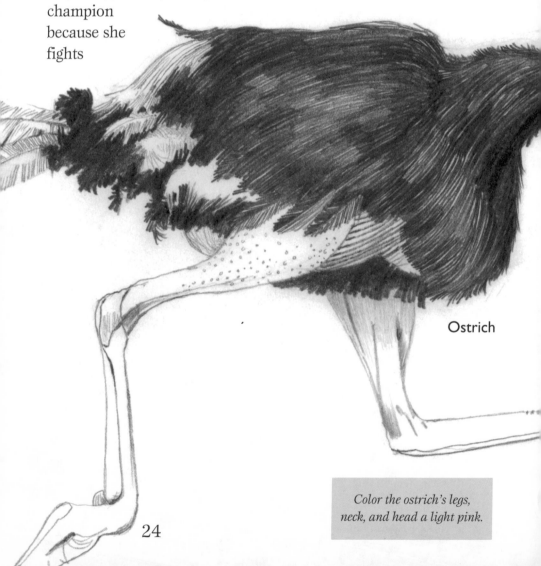

Ostrich

Color the ostrich's legs, neck, and head a light pink.

with her feet and can kill an enemy with one kick. BUT . . . this bird can't fly!

The ostrich is a strange-looking bird, with a round, fat body, skinny legs, a long neck, a small head, and big eyes that always look a little surprised. Maybe she IS surprised because she's a bird that can't fly!

But even though she can't fly, God sure made her move fast. When she's just walking, she goes about two miles an hour. When she gets startled, she runs 20 miles an hour, and when she gets really scared she can run 45 miles an hour!

Most people think an ostrich likes to bury her head in the sand, but that isn't really true. When the ostrich is resting or nesting, she may lay her long neck and head on the sand. And when she is eating, her small head almost disappears in the sandy grass. From a distance, she might LOOK like she has buried her head, but an ostrich would never be silly enough to do that.

The ostrich IS silly enough to swallow strange things. When she is living in her natural habitat—a semi-desert area or grassland—she eats plants, flowers, and seeds, but if she is living somewhere like a zoo, she gets curious and swallows other things. During her lifetime, one ostrich swallowed a roll of camera film, three gloves, a comb, a pencil, a piece of rope, some coins, a gold necklace, a handkerchief, and a clock!

Now YOU would never be silly enough to bury your head OR to put something in your mouth that didn't belong there! You know that you should only put good things in your mouth—like pizza, popcorn, ice cream, or a toothbrush! "Chew" on this idea today—an ostrich is big but can't fly, and a hummingbird is tiny but CAN fly. Which would you rather be?

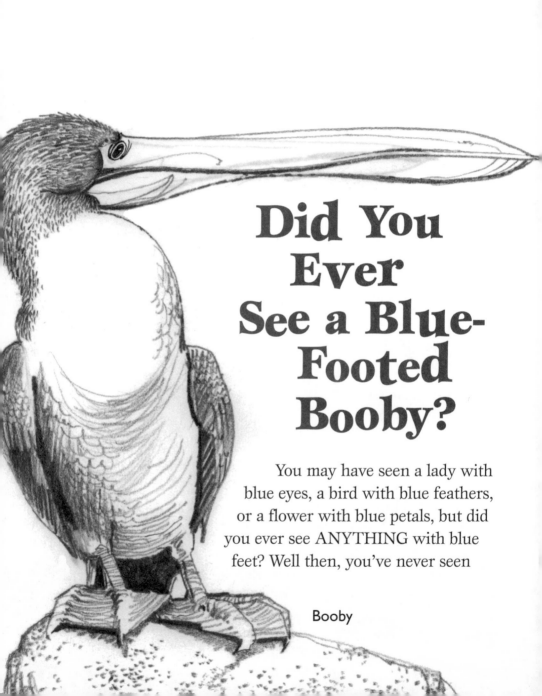

Did You Ever Ever See a Blue- Footed Booby?

You may have seen a lady with blue eyes, a bird with blue feathers, or a flower with blue petals, but did you ever see ANYTHING with blue feet? Well then, you've never seen

Booby

this bird! The booby is one of the most interesting looking—and most photographed—of all birds.

God gave the booby very big, bright blue feet that are webbed like a duck's feet. And the booby uses those feet to hatch baby boobies! Although most birds hatch their eggs by sitting or hovering over the eggs to keep them warm, the booby covers her eggs with her feet. Those big blue feet are very broad and warm and just the perfect size to cover the eggs.

The mommy and daddy boobies take turns "footing" the eggs until the baby chicks are hatched, and then the babies SIT on the parents' feet to keep warm until they are about a month old! The daddy booby goes fishing every day and brings back food for the baby chicks until they are old enough and strong enough to run around on their OWN bright blue feet!

Did YOU ever try walking or dancing by putting YOUR feet on the top of your mommy's or daddy's feet? It's fun to try, so why don't you ask some nice grown-up (like an aunt or a grandpa) to let you walk or dance on his or her feet today! Just hold on tight so you won't fall down, and giggle a lot as you think about those blue-footed birds who sit on their parents' feet. OR—every time you wear blue socks, pretend that you are a blue-footed bird and walk like a duck and think about all the different kinds of feet God made—cat feet, turkey feet, tiger feet, bear feet, and bare people-feet like yours!

You KNOW what color to make this bird's feet!

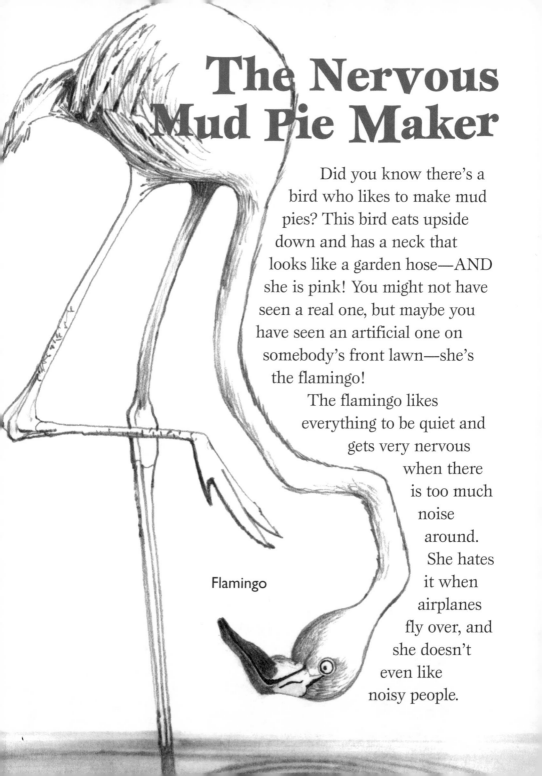

The Nervous Mud Pie Maker

Did you know there's a bird who likes to make mud pies? This bird eats upside down and has a neck that looks like a garden hose—AND she is pink! You might not have seen a real one, but maybe you have seen an artificial one on somebody's front lawn—she's the flamingo!

The flamingo likes everything to be quiet and gets very nervous when there is too much noise around. She hates it when airplanes fly over, and she doesn't even like noisy people.

Flamingo

The flamingo is tall with legs that look like long sticks. Halfway up her leg is a joint that looks like a knee, but it is actually an ankle. It bends BACKWARD when she sits down!

When the flamingo gets hungry, she stands in the water, and, since she is so tall, she has to bend her long neck way down into the water. Her beak is made like a scoop, and she puts her head in the water UPSIDE DOWN and scoops up a big mouthful of mud, hoping to find some shrimp or water plants in the mud for supper—and she usually does. Her scoop beak filters out the mud, and she eats the food, but she doesn't mind mud—she likes it. She even uses mud to build a nest—and the nest looks like a big mud pie!

The flamingo looks very unusual standing in the mud, but when she takes off and flies with a whole flock of other pink flamingos she is very graceful and the flock in flight is a beautiful sight to see.

Are you like the flamingo? Do you like to make mud pies? Does noise make you nervous? Sometimes noise can be fun but, just for today, pretend you are a flamingo and try to find a very quiet place to sit. And while you're being quiet, think of all the different and unusual kinds of birds God made—and think which bird acts the most like YOU do. It might be fun to be a bird and fly, but don't you think it's more fun being YOU?

Color the flamingo a bright pink.

Who Wears a Tuxedo to Go Sledding?

If you've ever been to a fancy wedding or party—or watched one on TV or in a movie—you might have seen men wearing black-and-white suits that are called tuxedos. This bird looks like he's wearing a fancy tuxedo all the time—even when he goes sledding!

Penguins have a waddling walk, and it's fun to watch a group of them marching along in a line, waddling back and forth across the ice. Then when they get to the top of a hill, they drop down on their stomachs and go sliding down the hill, zipping along as fast as a kid on a sled. Wouldn't you like to see the "tuxedo birds" sledding—WITHOUT a sled?

God made some penguins small and some tall. The emperor penguin is the biggest, and he is almost as tall as some bears. This penguin lives near the South Pole where it is always very, very cold, so he always walks on snow or ice or swims in cold water. Sometimes when the icy wind is very strong, the parents gather all the little penguins together and stand in a circle around them to make a "fence" of grown-ups.

But penguins LIKE the cold, rough sea. They are great swimmers, and they play in the waves and dive for food. But they do have a very strange way of getting OUT of the water. A penguin will dive down and then swim toward shore as fast as he can. Just before he gets to the land, he suddenly leaps high in the air (sometimes as high as six feet!) and always lands on the shore standing straight up on his feet. Wouldn't you like to see THAT landing!

Would YOU like to dress up in a tuxedo to go sledding—or swimming? Do you ever like to dress up in something different from what you usually wear? Maybe you have dressed up and pretended that you are somebody else—like an astronaut or a movie star or a bus driver or a zoo keeper? Maybe one day you will have one of those jobs, but whatever job you do—in the future OR today—do the best you can do. Then you can be proud of yourself and others will be proud of you too!

Since the penguin is black and white, color the ice a very pale blue.

Penguin

Taking a Bath with Ants?

This bird is so popular that songs, books, and poems have been written about him! One of the songs goes, "When the red, red robin comes bob, bob, bobbing along . . . ." Have you ever heard someone singing that song?

Of course, the robin isn't really red—just his chest feathers are red. People like the robin because he's the first bird that comes "bobbing" around in the spring, singing and digging for his favorite food—worms. BUT this bird also has a very strange habit known as "anting." When a robin "ants," he looks like he is taking a bath in ants! He looks very funny!

Sometimes the robin gets itchy skin (like you might if you have poison ivy or a rash). Since the robin can't go to the drugstore to get medicine, God has taught him to go to an ant hill! The robin lets the ants crawl all over him—and sometimes he will take an ant in his beak and "comb" it through his feathers. No one knows why this works, but there must be something on the ant that cures the itch!

Now here's another story about the robin that you can tell someone today.

Sing a song, bob along, and color this robin's chest flame red.

There's a legend that says when Joseph and Mary and the baby Jesus were traveling to Egypt, they had to camp out at night. It was very cold, so they built a little fire of twigs. But when they went to sleep the fire started to go out. A robin saw what was happening, so he swooped down and flapped his wings to fan the flame and keep the fire burning. He spent all night long fanning the fire so the baby Jesus would stay warm.

In the morning, the feathers on the bird's chest had turned to an orangey-red color, like the color of the flames, because the bird had been by the fire so long. And ever since robins have had red chest feathers as a sign of the way that first robin took care of the baby Jesus. Of course, this is just a story, but isn't it a GOOD story?

Robin

33

Flicker

The Drummer with a Mustache

Did you know that God made a bird who looks like he's wearing a mustache? He did! Some flickers have black mustaches and some have red ones—but they are all drummers! The flicker will "drum" or tap on a dead branch, a TV antenna, a tin roof, or anything that will make noise and "broadcast" his drumming.

The flicker also likes to picnic. When people go on a picnic and sit on the grass, ants sometimes invite themselves to join in, and they get all over the food. The flicker gets even. He likes to sit on the grass and have a picnic by eating the ANTS!

The flicker has a strange call that sounds like "wick, wick, wick" or "flicka, flicka, flicka." AND he has a stiff tail that he uses to prop himself up on the side of a tree! The flicker does NOT like the busy cities. He can be happy in the country or the suburbs, but the flicker is NOT a city slicker!

Which do YOU like best—the city, the country, or in between? Where would you like to live someday—in a noisy, hurry-up city that is very exciting or in a quiet, country place where you could go on a picnic whenever you want? Or maybe you would like to become a drummer in a band and travel to all KINDS of places!

Make yourself a drum today out of an empty oatmeal box or a round pot from the kitchen—OR make up a song using "wick, wick, wick" or "flicka, flicka, flicka"—OR go through an old magazine and draw mustaches on the pictures of all the people. While you are drumming or singing or drawing, think about how much fun God must have had when he painted a mustache on a bird!

Color the flicker's wing and tail yellow.

The Condominium Martins

Here's a bird who likes to live in a condo or an apartment house! Most bird families nest in one little house, but the purple martin likes lots of company and moves into a multi-family "martin house" that is built high in the air on a pole! When they first arrive at the house, some of the martins fuss and squawk about who gets which apartment, but once they settle down they nest happily and make good neighbors.

The purple martins make good neighbors for people, too, because God gave these birds a strange appetite. They like to eat flies, mosquitoes, wasps, beetles, and other bugs—and they eat LOTS of them. That makes people happy because the martins keep all those pesky bugs out of their yards.

The Choctaw and Chickasaw Indians were probably the first to notice that the martins would make good neighbors and that they liked to live together. The Indians strung up rows and rows of hollowed-out

Martin

gourds to lure the birds to come and nest in their villages. When farmers saw this, they copied the idea and built the first bird "apartment houses."

The martins eat "on the wing," catching mosquitoes or other insects in the air while flying along. They also get a drink or bath "on the wing" by swooping down to dip into a stream or pond to grab a drink or a quick dunk-bath.

And when the martins fly off to spend the winter in a warmer spot, they still like company. Sometimes as many as 100,000 birds will fly together in one flock. And when they stop to rest for the night, there are so many of them that they often break the branches of a tree!

Would you like to see a big flock like that? It would look like a big black cloud! The next time there's a storm and you see a big black cloud, think of the martins and thank God for making such good neighbors.

Although this bird is named the purple martin, it really isn't purple. It's a glossy blue-black that looks sort of purple in the sunshine, so why don't you color the BIRDHOUSE purple!

The Secret Hideaway Surprise

Hornbill

Many birds have interesting ways of building homes, but you will be surprised when you hear about the hornbill's hideaway! The hornbills look around until they find a nice, big hole in a tree, and they build a nest inside the hole. Then the mommy bird climbs into the hole, and they SEAL UP the front of the hole with mud, leaving just a tiny opening big enough for the mommy bird's beak to stick out. The mud will harden like plaster, and the mommy bird will stay sealed INSIDE for a long time—sometimes for THREE months.

While the mommy bird hatches the eggs inside the nest, the daddy bird comes and feeds her and the baby birds. Hurrying around looking for food makes the daddy bird tired and thin, and his tail feathers get all shaggy from rubbing against the tree bark all the time. And when the mommy bird finally breaks out of her sealed-in nest, she will be fat and stiff from staying in such a small place for so long. But the babies will be healthy and happy and sometimes they will even try to seal themselves back into their secret snug nest home. But not the mommy bird! She is very glad to be out in the world again!

Aren't the hornbills smart? Their strange home protects their babies without a burglar alarm! No enemy could get inside such a secret sealed-up nest!

Pretend you are a bird and need to build a nest. Would you build it way up high or down low so you could find food more easily? Would you seal it up or leave it open and airy so you could feel the breeze and flap your wings? Isn't it exciting that God made the birds so different and that they build so many different kinds of homes—just like people do!

Color this bird's bill and that strange knob on top of his bill yellow.

The "Good Luck" Bird

In many cities in Europe you can see VERY big bird nests high on the rooftops. The birds nesting there are big, white storks. The people like to have them nest there because they think storks bring good luck to their homes. And besides, it's fun to have another family living on your roof!

The storks have very long legs and very long beaks. When they have babies in the nest, either the mommy bird or the daddy bird will stay to watch the babies while the other one goes off to look for food.

Stork

The one who stayed at home will watch the sky, waiting for the other stork to come home safely. When the food-shopper DOES get home, the stork who stayed behind stands up and rattles its beak. The other stork rattles its beak right back. And then they politely bow to each other!

The storks rattle their beaks to "talk" or communicate. They are very happy "family" birds. BUT the stork is one bird that does not sing or chirp or make any sound—because it has no voice!

Aren't you glad YOU have a voice so you can sing and talk and giggle and shout "yoo-hoo" when someone comes home whom you are glad to see?

If you have a tape recorder, pretend today you are a reporter. Go around and ask people questions and record their answers. Then play the tape back and listen to see how different each person's voice sounds. If you DON'T have a tape recorder, you can still go around and ask questions and just LISTEN to see how each voice is different. Then say a prayer to thank God for your voice to talk, your ear to listen, and your mind to learn about polite birds like the stork!

Color the storks' beak and long legs orange.

Who-o-o Said That?

The wise old owl has such big, staring eyes, he seems to be asking "WHO?" even when he isn't hooting "Hooo, Hooo!" God made the owl's eyes VERY large to let in lots of light so the owl can see to hunt in the dark. BUT the owl's eyes are so large, there is no room for them to move around the way YOUR eyes do. This means the owl can only look STRAIGHT AHEAD, not sideways or up and down.

But that's OK. God also gave the owl a twisty neck so when the owl is watching something move, his head seems to turn all the way around and upside down! Sometimes it looks like his head will twist right off!

And that's not all. This bird also has very unusual ears. One ear is bigger and higher than the other so it can hear low-pitched noises—like a dog growling. The smaller ear is "tuned" to hear high-pitched sounds—like a pig squealing. With these ears the owl can hear the very faintest sound in the deep black darkness of the night.

Check to see how YOUR eyes work today. Look to the right, to the left, up, down, and all around WITHOUT moving your head. Now look ONLY straight ahead like the owl and twist your whole head around as far as you can to see like the owl does. Of course, if you want to look BEHIND you, you'll have to get a mirror and walk around looking in it so you can see where you've been!

Neither you NOR the owl can see everything everywhere. Only God can do that! Doesn't it make you feel good to know that God can see everything and is watching over you WHEREVER you go?

Color the owl's big eyes bright yellow.

Owl

43

One Good Tern Deserves Another!

This bird is called the Arctic tern, but sailors once called them "sea butterflies" because of the way they fly—bouncing and fluttering around in a way that makes you think of butterflies.

They may be bouncy flyers, but they take longer trips than almost any other bird or animal. They spend the winter in the Antarctic because it is easier to find food there, but in the springtime they fly north of the Arctic circle to make nests and hatch new little terns. And do you know how long that round-trip flight is? To go to the Arctic circle and then back again, the terns fly about 20,000 miles! They could certainly qualify for a "frequent fliers" club.

If you could fly like a bird, you could go all the way around the world by flying 25,000 miles—and these birds fly almost that far every year! Of course, they always go to and from the same place—so they may be frequent flyers, but they only see two places each year!

Would YOU like to fly around the world someday—not like a bird but on an airplane so you could stop and get off and visit some of the wonderful cities and countries in the world? Would you like to go to the cold Arctic to ride a dogsled across the ice

Tern

and snow
and see
the
"sea
butterflies"—
or would you like to go to
a warm seaside where you
could soak in the sun and see
real butterflies flit around the
flowers?

Wasn't it nice of God to make so many
different places and so many different things for
frequent flyers to visit and explore? Wouldn't it be nice if
you said a little prayer to thank him
for that today?

*The tern is black and white,
so color the sky blue—and
leave a little white cloud.*

45

The Trash Collector

Some people like small homes; some people like big ones. Some birds like small nests—but the osprey likes a re-e-eally big nest. Most birds build a new nest every year, but the osprey comes back year after year, adding more and more to the same nest—and that's why it gets SO big. The nest is usually in a tree or on a high "shelf" large enough to hold a really big nest. Although the osprey starts out by building the nest with sticks and twigs, she keeps adding bits and pieces of other things. Ospreys have been known to add such things as bath towels, old rubber boots, and even straw hats to their huge trash-filled nests!

Osprey

In some bird families the lady bird and the gentleman bird look alike, but in others they have different-colored feathers. The ospreys have the same colors, except for one difference. The lady osprey has a "necklace" of brown streaks on the feathers of her chest. Isn't that fun—a lady bird with a necklace!

Does somebody in your family sometimes think you are like the osprey—because wherever you go, you leave a jumble of stuff that looks like the osprey's trash-filled nest? Maybe today would be a good day to un-osprey your house by picking up and putting away all the toys and clothes and dishes you have left somewhere they are not supposed to be! Or maybe you could volunteer to take out the trash today!

And then make up an osprey prayer. It might go like this:

Thank you, Lord, for all the funny things
the osprey to her nest might bring.
But, Lord, don't let me be
like the osprey!
Help me to do my best
to keep a clean nest.
Amen.

*Color the leaves of the
tree green.*

Beep!
Beep!

Did you ever see a roadrunner cartoon on TV where the sly and speedy bird dashes about saying "Beep! Beep!"? Well, did you know God made a REAL bird called the roadrunner? This bird lives in the desert, and he really DOES speed down the road or across the desert like the bird in the cartoon. And he looks very funny because he will race along and then, without "signaling," speedily zoom to the right or turn to the left or suddenly STOP for just a second and then race off again—like a crazy driver in one of those car-chase scenes in the movies.

Do you know how the roadrunner can make such quick stops and turns? God gave him a long black tail to use like a BRAKE when he wants to stop and to use for a rudder when he wants to make a sudden turn. Who needs a movie stunt car when you have a tail like that!

And guess where the roadrunner builds his nest. He builds a saucer-shaped nest and puts it right in the middle of a cactus plant! Did you ever see a cactus? It has sharp prickly little thorns all over it, so it does NOT seem like a very friendly place to build a home. But since there are lots of cactus plants in the desert and very few trees, the cactus must seem like the perfect home-sweet-home spot to the speedy roadrunner.

Have you ever met people who remind you of a cactus? They act all prickly like they're in a bad mood all the time, and sometimes they use sharp or mean words. Now YOU would never act like a cactus would you?

If you have ever done that, tell God you're sorry—and then run fast like a roadrunner to the person you treated in an unkind way and give that person an "I'm sorry" and un-prickly hug.

The roadrunner is gray and black, so color the cactus green.

Roadrunner

The Curly-Haired Curassow

When you take a first look at this bird you might think she has naturally curly hair, since the top of her head is covered with curly ringlets. The "curls" are actually fancy little feathers that make the curassow look like she is always having a "good-hair day"!

This bird's unusual name sounds like the name of Curacao Island (which is far away in the Dutch Indies), but no one has ever seen a curassow in Curacao! Instead, this bird lives in Mexico and parts of South America.

The curassow is a large bird, about the size of a turkey. She finds her food—fruit and leaves—on the ground, but she flies into a tree to roost and rest. This is a rain forest bird, and she is probably very proud of her beautiful head of curls and would not want anyone to know that she is a distant relative of the plain, ordinary chicken! Shhhh. Don't tell.

Do you ever have trouble with YOUR hair? When you wake up in the morning, do you ever look like you've been out in a wind storm—with your hair sticking up or out in all directions?

Do you ever go and get your hair cut, and it gets cut all wrong?
Would you rather have purple hair or green hair or curly
feathers on top of your head like the curassow?
God gave you just the kind of hair that looks best
on YOU, and even if it doesn't always curl
or not curl the way you might wish,
when God looks at you he thinks you
look just perfect—because that's the
way he made you!

The curassow is black and white, but if you want to color her hair green go right ahead!

Curassow

Who Ever Heard of a Secretary Bird?

Secretary Bird

Have you ever seen a teacher put a pencil behind her ear—so she'd know just where to find it when she needed to write something? Sometimes a secretary will also stick a pencil in her hair just behind her ear so she will have the pencil handy when the boss calls and asks her to take down a note.

A long time ago, instead of using a pencil, a secretary would write with something called a quill pen. This pen was made out of a feather and would be used by dipping the sharp end of the feather into ink. And do you know what? The first person who spotted this bird saw those feathers standing up behind its head, thought she looked like she had stuck a couple of quill pens behind her ear, and called it a secretary bird! And it's been called that ever since.

Did you ever get a letter or a birthday card where somebody wrote your name in pencil? Or maybe you have seen your name written with pen or crayon. But did you know that you could "send a message" WITHOUT using a pencil or a pen or a crayon? You CAN when you want to send a message to God! Why don't you think about what you would like to tell God today? Then pretend you are a secretary writing a letter to God! You don't even have to mail this kind of letter, because God will know what it says!

The secretary bird looks like she is wearing RED eye shadow, so color just a bit of red above her eyes.

The DecOratOr Weaver

Did you ever decorate your house for a party by hanging crepe paper streamers and balloons all over—or did you ever watch somebody else do that? Well, did you know that God made weaverbirds, who like to decorate TREES with their nest? Sometimes a tree will be so full of weaverbird nests that it will look like it is full of balloons!

It isn't easy for a little bird to weave a nest like this. The weaverbird has to learn how to do it just like you would have to learn how to knit a sock or weave a basket. Young weavers build "practice" nests that often fall apart! And they have to start all over again. But they keep trying—weaving straw in and out until they get a nest that is just right. And weaverbirds like to get together, so a whole bunch of them will build nests in one tree.

Weaverbirds are also very careful birds and like to build somewhere safe from anyone who might try to hurt their babies. So you know what they do? They can't go out and buy a burglar alarm, so they build their nests near a beehive or a wasp

nest, since birds are safe from bee bites and wasp stings—but people are not! Aren't those weaverbirds smart?

The next time you have to learn how to do something NEW and have to keep starting over, OR the next time you have to do something HARD that takes lots of practice, remember the weaverbirds—and keep trying until you get it just right!

Weaverbird

Color the weaverbird nests the color of straw and the tree green.

The Acrobat Bird

Here's a friendly little bird you may have met right in your own backyard. She is easy to spot because when God dressed this bird, he decided she should wear a black "cap" and a black "bib" or scarf on her white feathers.

The little chickadee sings her own name, chirping "chick-a-dee-dee-dee" as she nibbles at the neighborhood bird feeders. And if you watch her, you'll see her do all kinds of "acrobatic" acts at the feeder. She'll reach under and around and through a branch and sometimes even hang

Chickadee

56

UPSIDE DOWN to grab a tasty snack.

Do you ever wear a scarf or some kind of cap—a baseball cap, a warm wool cap for the winter, or a silly cap just for fun? Maybe you would like to put on your "thinking" cap or your "do-something-different" cap today and make a little bird feeder to hang up for the chickadees. It's easy to do.

You could just take a bagel and toast it and spread it with peanut butter. Then put a ribbon through the bagel hole and hang it from a bush or tree. OR here's another idea . . . Take an empty half-pint milk carton (like the kind you get at school or at a restaurant) and wash it out. Push the spout back in and punch a little hole in the top "handle" big enough to string a ribbon through. Now totally COVER the carton with creamy peanut butter (except for the top where the hole is). Drop the carton into a bag where you have put some bird seed or some crispy cereal. Close the bag and shake it carefully until the carton is completely covered with seeds or cereal. Take your bird-house-shaped bird feeder and put a ribbon or string through the hole and hang it outside. Now watch from a window and see if one of God's chickadee acrobats will show up to do some tricks for you.

Since this is another black-and-white bird, color the branch brown.

Here Comes a Parade!

Did you ever watch a parade coming down the street with a band marching along? The leader of the band usually steps very high and wears a very high hat—and that hat sometimes has a big decoration right on top. Well, this bird looks like he's wearing one of those hats!

When God made the quail, he gave him a bunch of feathers right on top of his head, feathers that stand straight up and bob back and forth as the quail hurries along. The quail has lots of energy and is always on the run, like people bustling about on a busy city street. Maybe that's why his "song" sounds like he is singing "Chi-CAH-go!"

These pretty, plump birds often live in a wooded area where there is "underbrush"—weeds or plants that are easy to hide in. The male quail will venture out first, looking all around to see if this is a safe place to stop for lunch. He will pace back and forth nervously—again, looking like he's in a parade. Once he decides it's safe, he invites his wife to come and join him.

If they find a safe backyard, they sometimes become quite friendly with the people who live there. But the quail are shy, and if they hear a scary sound they will hurry away with a twittering whir of wings.

Sometimes you will see only a pair of quail together, but at other times you will see a group (or covey) of ten to twenty quail marching along, waving their plumed hats—on parade!

Would you like to travel to a big city like Chicago? You could "make believe" you are traveling there today! Find some cardboard boxes and put them in a row like the cars of a train. Ask some friends to "ride" along, one in each box, and then you can tell each other all the things you "see" from the "train" as you travel! MAYBE you could ask someone to teach you the words to the quail's song, "Chi-cah-go, Chi-cah-go, it's my kind of town . . . ," and then sing that song as you "ride" along!

The quail is black and white, so use your imagination to color this page!

Quail

Mockingbird

The Dive Bomber Borrower Bird

This bird likes to "dive bomb" dogs and cats—and some-times people! And he also "borrows" songs from other birds!

Meet the mockingbird—a bird who wears PLAIN gray and black feathers with just a touch of white on the wing but has a VERY COLORFUL personality.

60

Did you ever see a comedian on TV who can change his voice so he will sound just like the voice of some other person? Well, God gave this bird a voice that can do that too. The mockingbird seems to "borrow" the sounds of other birds so he can add their songs to his. And he LOVES to sing!

He will sit on a high perch and sing for hours, sounding like ALL the other birds in his neighborhood. Sometimes he will even imitate OTHER sounds like a squeaky bicycle wheel, a frog, a chicken, an alarm clock, a piano, or a barking dog! A mockingbird once got everybody's attention and caused a traffic jam by making the sound of a police whistle over and over!

Known as the "many-tongued mimic," this bird also likes to tease dogs and especially cats. Just for fun—or sometimes to scare off an "enemy" cat or person—he will swoop down in a fast dive and look like he is going to run his beak right into the "target." At the last second, he pulls out of the dive and flies around, waiting to see if he has scared off the "enemy." If his attack didn't work, he will dive-bomb again and again.

This is a bird who is never without something interesting to do. If he isn't singing or diving, he will jump off his high perch and do a somersault in the air. Or he will visit a berry bush for a snack. (He also likes raisins, donuts, AND cottage cheese!)

Did YOU ever sing or do somersaults or pretend to "dive bomb" an "enemy"? Or have you ever eaten cottage cheese? Try out YOUR voice today and see if you can sound like somebody else. If you could be "many-tongued" like the mockingbird, whose voice would you MOST like to sound like?

Since the mockingbird does not LOOK colorful, color the berries red.

61

The Parking Lot Bird

Most birds spend a lot of time and do a lot of work to build snug and sometimes fancy nests—but not this bird. This bird has the strange name of killdeer, but she does NOT kill deer and she does NOT build a nest!

The killdeer just lays her eggs

Killdeer

right on the bare ground or on a flat gravel roof or EVEN on a gravel parking lot! She guards her eggs fiercely against passersby—which is not easy in a parking lot! When somebody gets near her nest, she will run out, dragging her wing to act like she is hurt—to draw attention away from her eggs.

Since God made this nest-less bird, he also made sure that her baby birds would be ready to run the minute they are hatched. And, since these birds likes to eat bugs instead of berries, when they leave the parking lot they head for a nearby marsh or brook where they can find a bug-gy lunch. It isn't too hard for them to do this because the mother bird chooses a parking lot or roof that is near a lakeshore, riverbank, or stream of water.

Although you might think this should be called "the gravel bird," it gets its strange name because the call it makes SOUNDS like "kill-deer."

Aren't you glad you were born in a hospital instead of in a parking lot?

Did you ever see a story on TV about a baby being born in a parking lot? Instead of watching a story on TV today, make up your OWN story! Make up a story about a bird who lives in a parking lot. What will you name the mommy bird? What will you name the baby birds? And what adventures will they have? Maybe you can get a friend or somebody who lives in your house to HELP you make up the story. And while you're imagining your story, remember that people can make stories AND parking lots—but only God can make a funny bird like the killdeer!

Color the gravel brown or gray.

The Blue Bower Builder

The bowerbird does not build a nest—he builds a house! At least that is what it looks like. When explorers in New Guinea first saw a bowerbird's house, they thought it must have been built by children to use as a playhouse. They couldn't believe a BIRD could build something like that. But the bowerbird did!

Some of these "bird houses" have roofs. Some have rooms. And they are ALL decorated. There are several different kinds of bowerbirds, and they build different kinds of houses. One bowerbird uses twigs to build a house around a tree. His house looks like a thatched hut and can be over six feet tall—taller than a tall man!

Then the bowerbird uses moss to make a "garden" in front of his house, and he decorates it with shells, berries, stones, and flowers. And when the flowers die, he throws them out and brings in fresh flowers so his garden will always look bright and pretty.

The blue satin bowerbird uses sticks to build two tall walls like an "arch" that he and his wife can walk through—stepping on a "carpet" of soft twigs. He decorates HIS house too, but his idea of something pretty is something BLUE, so EVERYTHING he puts in his house is blue—a blue feather, a blue berry, a blue flower. And you won't believe what he does next! He makes a "paintbrush" out of a piece of bark, holds the bark in his

64

mouth, and dips it in "paint" made of blue berry juice. Then the blue satin bowerbird PAINTS the walls of his bower blue!

How do you think these birds learned to build houses or knew how to decorate them? And how did one learn to like ONLY the color blue? Do you guess maybe God taught them?

What has God taught YOU? If you listen closely, maybe you will hear God teaching you that it is WRONG to lie or steal or disobey your parents, but it is RIGHT to be happy and to keep in your heart the message that God loves you and is your friend.

Bowerbird

Color the bowerbird's decorations the way you think the bowerbird would color them.

The Showoff "Fan Club"

Of all the birds, this one probably has the most beautiful feathers, AND it is the only one who can do an amazing "fan dance." You could also say that this bird belongs to a men-only fan club! That's because only the daddy peacock owns a fascinating, fabulous, many-colored fan.

Peacock

The peacock usually walks along quietly, dragging his tail behind him—and his tail is very long. It looks a bit like the long beautiful "train" of material that is attached to the back of a lady's fancy wedding dress.

But THEN the peacock suddenly does something surprising and stupendous. He lifts that long tail and spreads out the feathers until he looks like he is standing in front of a huge fancy fan! The fan shimmers in the light with lots of colors, and it has a dazzling design that MIGHT make you think lots of beautiful eyes are looking at you!

The peacock also shakes his "fan," and the feathers make a loud rustling sound. Then he prances about, walks like a soldier on parade, and sometimes does a little dance. He wants to get your attention. He wants you to notice how handsome he is!

Because the peacock is so proud of his feathers, we sometimes say a person who is bragging or excited or pleased about something is "proud as a peacock."

Now why do you think God made a bird with a fan for a tail? Maybe God wanted to get YOUR attention. You might not notice a quiet little bird in your backyard tree, but you couldn't help but notice a peacock if you saw one at the zoo. Maybe God wants you to notice BOTH! God made some birds beautiful and some plain, some noisy and some quiet—just like he made people different. But God made each bird and each person in a SPECIAL way, and he wants YOU to notice each one and love each one just like he does.

Color the peacock's body dark blue, his tail green, and the tail "eyes" yellow with purple and greenish-blue centers.

Funny Fowl Facts

What ELSE would you like to know about the birds God made? Did you know birds are sometimes called "fowl"? Did you know it takes 25,000 feathers to cover a swan and 950 feathers just to cover the little ruby-throated hummingbird? Did you know the hummingbird has 14 tiny bones in its neck? (That's TWICE as many bones as there are in a giraffe's neck!) Did you know there are about 100,000 MILLION birds in the world—but 3,000 million of them are chickens?! Here are some more questions and answers about God's feathered friends:

How Do Birds Fly?

Would you believe that birds have different ways of flying the same way people have different ways of walking? Some people walk ve-e-ery slowly; others walk so fast you can hardly keep up with them. Some people shuffle their feet; others march like a soldier. Some take little steps; others take big ones.

Well, birds are different too. Some birds dip and climb, while others lurch this way and that. Some birds fly swift and straight as an arrow, while others skim, soar, flap their wings slowly and steadily, or take quick flaps and then coast for a while.

Some birds are like airplanes. Gulls, albatrosses, and vultures are like sailplanes. Hummingbirds hover like a helicopter. Grouse take off with a burst of speed but don't last long, while ducks take off more slowly but can fly for long distances.

How Do Birds Sound?

To you, all bird songs may sound alike, but birds do not all have the same "voice." Birds whistle, warble, buzz, trill, tweet, cheep—and the bearded bell bird "chimes" like a bell. The mockingbird makes ALL of those sounds!

Some birds even seem to say their own names—the chickadee, the bobwhite, the whippoorwill, the killdeer, and others.

Where Do Birds Live?

Some birds build their own nests; others like to move into a ready-built birdhouse. Some birds build nests in strange places—in a flowerpot, a mailbox, an old tin can, or even the pocket of a scarecrow's shirt!

Some birds live only in one part of the country. (A Baltimore oriole would not be found in California, and a Canada jay would not be sighted in New Jersey—unless they got lost or flew away from home!) But some birds live in lots of places and lots of different countries all over the world, so you might see them almost anywhere.

How Does a Bird Act?

Some birds hop; some walk. Some birds flit about nervously; others sit quietly. Some birds make friends with people; others fly away and hide as soon as they see anybody who is not wearing feathers. Woodpeckers are great tree climbers. Nuthatches climb trees too—but backwards! They start at the top and climb DOWN, going head first!

How Do Birds Look?

Some birds look a lot alike except for the colors of their feathers. Others are VERY different—in size, shape, the type of beak, and the type of "markings." Some have long sharp beaks; others have big blunt beaks. Some have special markings around the eyes—lines or stripes or circles. Some have markings that make them look like they're wearing a collar or a hat. Some have long tails, and some have short bob-tails. Some have special "designs" on their wings.

In that way, birds are like people, who also come in different sizes and shapes, have different kinds of beaks (or noses) and eyes of different colors. Of course, people don't have wings. Only birds—and angels—have those!

Here are some other bird tidbits:

- You can find birds almost everywhere—down in coal mines, up on mountain tops, in green jungles and dry deserts, flying over oceans, and roosting in your backyard.

- Some birds are smaller than moths; some are taller than people.

- The ostrich lays an egg so big it would equal eighteen chicken eggs, and it would take 40 minutes to soft boil it!

- A bird known as a "swift" can fly in his sleep! He rises high in the sky when the sun is going down and sleeps on the wing. Then he lands at dawn!

- A bird called a cassowary wears a "crash helmet." He has a flattened, horny crown on the top of his head that protects him when he runs crashing through thick underbrush.

- Looking like they're in a "water ballet," western grebes will rush two-by-two across a pond or lake. Powered by their splashing feet, they seem to be walking on water!

- High on a tree branch the "greater treeswift" glues pieces of bark together to make a cup just large enough for ONE egg. This is one of the smallest bird nests in the world.

- A group of social "weaverbirds" builds a stiff straw "roof" all across the top of a tree and then adds tunnels where they can nest and each family can have its own "door" to get in. The roof is waterproof, and the birds live there all year long. Some of these nests last for 100 years!

- Some geese and ducks run "nursery schools" where a few adult birds take care of dozens of the children of other birds. Some of the duck "schools" will have as many as 100 little ducklings!

- The woodcock's eyes are BEHIND ITS EARS!

- The hummingbird breathes 250 times a minute!

- There is only ONE poisonous bird in the whole world and that is a rare bird with the rare name of the hooded pitohui.

- Some birds have really funny names—like the ririro (a New Zealand warbler), the zoozoo (a ringdover), and the seesee (a West Asian sand partridge).

Some birds "migrate" from a summer home to a winter home, traveling lo-o-ong distances. No one knows for sure how they find their way without a map, but they do! And sometimes they fly there very fast. Radar has recorded the speed of some birds and determined that most songbirds travel about 30 miles per hour (the speed limit for cars in city areas). Ducks can travel at almost 60 miles per hour (the speed limit for cars on lots of highways). Sandpipers can fly at 110 miles per hour. And swifts can fly up to 200 miles per hour (about as fast as most race cars go at the Indianapolis 500 race!).

There are so MANY things to learn about the birds God made. After you've read this book you may want to go to the library and find MORE books about birds. OR you may want to look for postage stamps that have pictures of birds on them and start a bird stamp collection. Or you may try to find out all the names of streets named for birds in your town and make a list of them. (One city has Hummingbird Street, Robin Wood Lane, Birdsong Avenue, Feather Drive, and lots more. You may be surprised at how many streets in YOUR city have bird-y names!)

Or you may want to say a prayer to thank God for all the birds and to say how happy you are to learn about his "colorful cavalcade of feathery friends!"